I0436932

They Took My Life and Left Me to Hang

DiPetri's story on how DYFS Took Him away and NEGLECTED Him.

Jamil V. Ellison

Bloomington, IN

authorHOUSE®

Milton Keynes, UK

AuthorHouse™
1663 Liberty Drive, Suite 200
Bloomington, IN 47403
www.authorhouse.com
Phone: 1-800-839-8640

AuthorHouse™ UK Ltd.
500 Avebury Boulevard
Central Milton Keynes, MK9 2BE
www.authorhouse.co.uk
Phone: 08001974150

First published by AuthorHouse 4/26/2007

ISBN: 978-1-4259-8592-9 (sc)

Printed in the United States of America
Bloomington, Indiana

This book is printed on acid-free paper.

This book is for: All those who said I couldn't.

Acknowledgments

I want to take a moment to thank the main factors, which helped me successfully complete my first book. First I have to give praise and thanks to God, my Father. If it wasn't for him I wouldn't be alive. I have been in quite a few near death experiences and I am still standing, so I knew God had a plan for me. I also want to thank my family, my mother and father, James and Evangeline Edwards, for always supporting me and caring for me. Even through all my hard and rough times, they stuck with me and I love them for that. My time away in a program helped me become wiser and taught me how to understand myself and how to do things for me. Just as I was that little boy who couldn't be helped by his friends, is now able to help him. Last but not least the spiritual people who have been in my life, Pastor Harvey, Mr. and Mrs. Harper, they helped me understand my Father much better, and how to come closer to Him. Lastly I want to thank my recent inspiration Yasmin C. Thanks to All!

Contents

Prologue

For anyone who reads this, be advised that this is not an ordinary chapter book—it has but two parts. It is a documentary of a child who has had bad experiences with foster families and overall life-changing events. This documentary includes a real-life autobiography, and the events and/or situations described are only those experienced by this child. Any type of information in this documentary is not meant to make anyone stop his or her normal life but to open the eyes of others who may have experienced the same neglect and abuse that this child has, as well as to open the eyes of those who need to see the type of life a confused child lives while in the system. This is a true story about a child who had gone through so many troubles and problems throughout his life. This little child was faced with many obstacles that he had no idea would cross his path and he couldn't push aside. His troubles ranged from losing a family of eight to facing terrible foster homes to being hit by a car. So let me express just what I know about this little child who is now trying to be all he can be in spite of his duress. Here's a little bit of knowledge about this remarkable young man.

Keep in mind that the names as well are false. No one's real name is used. But all information that follows is factual due to the author's personal experiences and or observations.

PART I

DIPETRI'S STORY

Early Childhood

It all started in my hometown of Elizabeth, New Jersey, where I was born on September 7, 1987, into a single-parent family of three at the Union County Hospital. I knew my mother but never my father. I do know that I kept having this dream that I had seen him. The picture remains vivid in my mind and I yearn to find out its meaning. I grew up in a terrible neighborhood, where there was violence and death left and right, and lived in a dangerous apartment building, where there were killings just about every night in the hallway. My mother moved us out of the apartment to another building that had one big apartment and an Arab landlord named Abu Baeda. Then the family grew and my mother had five more children, all of whom lived in the apartment, which seemed much smaller when there was a family of eight kids: Tom, Otis, DiPetri, Barry, George, Kim, Laura, and Trisha. My mother was very disturbed and extremely emotionally unstable when her own mother died. She just couldn't take the pressure, so she resorted to drugs and bad company to try to handle her stress. There were many times when we were dependent upon the oldest brother, Tom, who was at the time only twelve years old. Because our mother was away from home in the daytime, she'd leave Tom in charge. Wherever she would go, she'd always be back around or before 6:00 p.m. When she'd get home, she would expect for everything to be done and clean—meaning that we would have eaten a good dinner, the house was clean, and everyone was either taking baths or doing homework. Every night around eight p.m., after the baths and homework were completed, we all would sit around and watch scary shows like *Twilight* Zone and *Tales from the Crypt.* There were exceptions, of course: My mother sometimes returned home earlier than usual, then she'd take over.

We were very good in preschool and we learned a lot and listened to our teachers—sometimes. Otis and I ended up going to a disciplinary school called School 20. We never had much, and our mother was never around enough to teach us the basic do's and don'ts of life, so we had sort of developed that sense the hard way. Every day when we walked to school, we passed this little corner store across the street, and when I say little, I mean little—the dimensions must've been about ten by eighteen feet or thereabouts. Whenever we went in, we would go straight to a little section where there was candy, chips, Little Debbie's, Hostess cakes, Entenmann's pies and other snacks and we would shoplift one or two cakes apiece or a bag of chips and then we'd go to school—me to kindergarten and my brother to first grade. I think my brother was the mastermind, because when I tried shoplifting at the store once without him I got caught and chased. The first song I ever learned was in school, in my kindergarten music class, and that was "Sitting on the Dock of the Bay" by Otis Redding. I never had any trouble in preschool or kindergarten.

My mother soon remarried and our stepfather was very responsible and had a pretty good job, from which he was making enough to support a family of seven stepchildren, along with his new wife. One day the rest of the family were over at our house for a party and one of my aunts was touring the apartment while everyone else was in the kitchen eating, and then later she joined them. After the party, my mother said to my stepfather that my aunt had been in their room for a mighty long time, and they found that my aunt had stolen about seven hundred dollars from them. My mom told my stepfather to do something about it. A few days later my stepfather broke into my aunt's house and stole the money back, and of course she called the cops. She knew just who had done it because there was exactly seven hundred dollars missing, the amount she had stolen. My stepfather was sentenced to time in the state pen, and my family always went to visit him on set days and others we would yell at him through the window of his cell.

After I entered the first grade, I began to have many problems in school. My mother had become very violent toward my siblings and me and would often beat us. About once a week I would have to take home a note from my teacher saying how bad I had been in school, being disruptive in class and disrespectful to her. And every time, I would get a beating from Mom. After a while I stopped showing my mother the notes, but she found out anyway and wrote a letter to the teacher asking her to give any bad notes on me to her other son, Otis. Otis didn't fail to give the notes to our mother until he saw how sad and hurt I looked every time I got a beating. This sort of hurt his conscience and he accidentally or deliberately started forgetting to give the notes to our mother.

This went on for a while until Otis saw that I was getting way too many notes. He told me that hiding the notes would never make me do any better, instead it could hurt me. Then one day I was sent to the office for cursing at my teacher. While I was there, a little boy in kindergarten was sent in for pulling his pants down while I was in class. The principal dismissed me and told the child to pull his pants back down. She gave him a nice long beating with her wooden paddle. When I returned home, I found out that Otis had shown my mother another note about my bad behavior in school, and my mother gave me the most fierce and excruciating beating I have ever felt. She used a plunger stick, body-slammed me on the floor, and knocked my four front teeth out.

The next day when I went to school my teacher asked me what happened to me. I naively told her the truth, that my mom had beaten me. Soon enough, that teacher called the office, and the office called the Division of Youth and Family Services (DYFS). I was called down to the office, and when I got there, some social workers were waiting for me and asked me if I wanted to go with them or go home or stay in school. I said that I wanted to go home, and when I arrived my mother was there at the door crying. The last thing she told me was, "Promise that whatever happens, never change your name. You can add on whatever you'd like to it, but just please don't change it." Then DYFS came to take me away from my home. I was crying and watching my brothers and sisters cry as I rode away, and from that day on, I have never had any real respect for DYFS. I felt they could have done something else.

FAMILY ONE
Aunt Sable and Prizna of Roselle

I cried during the entire ride to the DYFS office, and I wanted nothing to do with any of the people there or with my caseworker. They tried to explain why I was there, but I just ignored them and sat there in anger while they were looking for a home for me to stay the night in. I stayed at the office until nightfall, when they found a home for me. They took me to Roselle to a nice-looking two-story house, whose caretakers were two old ladies who were sisters, one named Aunt Sable and the other named Prizna. When my caseworker tried to get me out of the car, I kicked, punched, and yelled at her at the top of my lungs, so that people from blocks around must have heard me. Well, it took about 4 days to get used to the drastic change, and even then I didn't respect the two women. My first night there, they locked me in my room for some reason unknown to me. I got to take a shower only once a week, on Sundays. They had taken in another kid, Bebe, who slept in the other bed in my room. After a while they took Bebe out of my room and let him sleep with Aunt Sable and then locked me in my room by myself. This could be a great hardship for me because sometimes in the middle of the night I really had to go pee, and my door was locked. Oftentimes I'd urinate on the floor, the wall, or out the window.   One day Aunt Sable saw the wall covered with urine and saw that under the bed there were many large, dark spots, and this really ticked her off. Immediately she called for me. When I came, she said, "What the hell is wrong with you? Is your bladder that damn weak?" I stood there and cried. She said, "I'm going to get you something to clean this up with," and she came back with a bucket of ammonia mixed with bleach and told me to get started. I was coughing, crying, choking, and vomiting while I knelt down breathing in the fumes of the two chemicals. My eyes were burning and my nose was stinging and felt like it was bleeding when it wasn't. Everytime I vomited, I was washing it in the chemicals, and I felt like I couldn't breathe. I would go to get air and Aunt Sable would say, "Get back down, boy, and clean!" This happened almost every time she watched me clean.

Then one night I urinated in her portable closet, where she kept her dry-cleaned clothes, because I didn't want to clean up the floor again and I'd really had to go. The next day Aunt Sable was looking for her dress that she had just brought home. When she looked in the closet and saw all of her cleaned clothes dirty and stinky, she gave me a little spanking and then told me to sit on the step. She told me that every day I was to sit on that step; I couldn't watch any TV and all I had to read were the same few little children's books. From that day on, I became an even more lonely and troubled child, because I had nobody to love and really care for me in my life, besides my mother, but I couldn't see her anymore. I didn't even have my foster parents to care for me; they disliked me a lot and wouldn't cater to my childhood needs.

So I found myself talking to myself a lot. My biggest fantasy was to grow up and have a wife, a nice car, and many kids. Every morning while I waited to be let out to sit on the step, I would make driving noises as if I were driving a minivan. In my imagination, we'd all get in and then I'd say, "Buckle up, kids, we're almost ready to roll." I didn't live an ordinary child's life. I was so eager to grow up and have a family. I had just barely started my life and already I wanted to be an adult and on my own. Forget toys and games and child things; I wanted greater.

Then there was my first nightmare, in which were these really hairy monsters that invaded my town, and the hairs on the monsters were extremely sharp. If you were stuck with one, you would become one of them. I said, "Come on, kids. Honey, let's go," and everybody in my imaginary family ran to our car. After I sat on one of the hairs, I noticed that the car was full of these hairy creatures. I screamed myself awake and Aunt Sable just said, "Shut up!" through the door and told me to go to sleep.

Aunt Sable and Prizna worked together at an optometrist's in a suite off of a major highway in North Jersey. It was still summer, so they took me to work with them every day. I had to sit in a little corner between the filing cabinet and the wall. Bebe was treated like a prize package—he was allowed to walk around the suite, and Prizna even walked around the entire building with him so he could see all the stores. Near the end of my stay, Prizna took me to the company banquet. I had to sit at the table where there were absolutely no people. I think if a person even came up to say hi or talk to me and treat me like a normal child, they would've moved me as soon as they could.

In about August I planned to run away because I knew that I had to get away from them. So while Prizna was giving me my shower on Sunday, I was thinking about how I was going to get out of there, and it came to me: Jump out of the window. After all, my window was only about two feet off the ground. I woke up around 7:30 a.m., put on my clothes, took my little Tonka truck, and took off down the hill. I was running like a bat out of hell and I was pretty lucky to be able to escape that easily because I had left so early in the morning, before Aunt Sable and Prizna woke up to get ready to go to work.

I ran through the projects. Once I reached the outskirts of town, I was feeling kind of hungry and stopped at a store. I didn't have any money, but I went in anyway. Only the store owner was there at the time, and he asked me if I was hungry. Of course I said yes. The store owner said, "Well, my name is Johnny Procter," and he fed me and gave me some snacks to take with me. Finally, John asked, "Kid, where are you heading?"

I said, "I'm heading home."

He replied, "Do you need a ride?" I said yes, and John called the police to pick me up. This was one of the greatest things that ever happened to me. The policeman drove me to my home on 355 East Jersey Street in Elizabeth. Along the way he let me play with the sirens and lights. When I got home, my mom and my brothers and sisters were there waiting for me. Before I could reach the door, the officer had a call about a runaway and he grabbed me before I reached my mom's outstretched arms. I cried and cried all the way back. Not only did I get separated from my family again, but I had to ride in the back this time. DYFS never came to see why I ran away, and probably didn't even know. The officer pulled up to my foster home and there was another squad car there, and police were standing in my room. Aunt Sable was still in her nightgown, having probably just woken up. The police were saying something that I wasn't even paying attention to, because I was too busy memorizing the route we had taken from home so I could use it to get back there again.

After that episode, Aunt Sable decided she'd better be more careful, so she took my pants and underwear before I went to bed and left me with only a shirt. They also took all of my clothes out of the room. The next morning I didn't care—I jumped out of the window anyway, barefoot and all, and headed home via the route as I remembered it. There was a guy walking down the street with me and he said he was going to take me to the police station to get clothes. I looked across the street at the police station and I followed him. Then Aunt Sable pulled up next to me, not long after I had left, and thanked the guy for trying to help me. Then they started talking about church and saying hi to people. DYFS still never came, not even for a month.

My birthday came around and I don't remember getting a cake or even a little party. I don't remember it being any type of celebration, just another day. So, for years afterward, I never told anyone my birthday—if they found out, oh well; but for me it will always be just another day.

Thanksgiving came around and I had to stay in my room and clean all day long. The floor and my ripped clothes smelled of damp wood being smoked. It was dark in my room because I didn't have a light switch there. The only light came from under the door. I stayed under the bed scrubbing nothing but dry floor; I knew that if Aunt Sable caught me not scrubbing, I would be in danger. I looked under the door and saw her family around the table and Bebe sitting next to her. I was waiting to be called out to join them, but that didn't happen until there was only one person left and it had to be around ten or eleven p.m. When she finally brought me out, they fixed a plate for me and told me that I was to only eat and then go back to my room. I truly felt like an outcast.

The food there was as good as the treatment; horrible. Every morning before school they'd have my breakfast waiting for me in the boiler room, where the washing machines were, in the basement. I never ate at the regular kitchen table, with Bebe. My food was hard or soggy; cold foods would sometimes be warm, and hot foods cool. I hated living there; I couldn't watch TV or play any games, I could only eat and go back to the room, and many weekends I wasn't fed breakfast or lunch at all. As a kid I loved going to school, because it was there that I felt like a normal human, not a caged animal. I felt and still feel today that my second-grade teacher and principal loved or cared more about me than my foster parents. Every morning before school, I'd have mushy cereal, a warm glass of milk (rarely did I get juice), and a piece of burnt toast. Then they'd send me off.

One day on the bus, a kid tried to stab me and I kicked him and he fell and dropped his knife. The school suspended me from the bus and I had to walk to school because Aunt Sable wasn't going to drive me. One day while walking to school I was very hungry and I stopped in this diner. The owner came up and asked where I was headed. I told him where and that I was hungry. When he asked why, I told him about the food I was getting. He then told me to have a seat at any table. When I sat down, a waitress brought me a strawberry-banana smoothie and a plate of pancakes, eggs, and bacon. I thanked the owner and they wrapped it up into a sandwich for me. The owner told me that I could come back any time and he would leave a note for whoever was on duty. So I went every morning.

I could have sworn my foster parents hated me, because anything good I wanted, they'd deny it. A school trip came up once and everyone got permission slips to take home. On my way to my foster parents' house, I began to feel dreary and depressed. I knew that they wouldn't allow it, and they wouldn't sign or pay for it. I chanced it anyway, and I was right—they refused. I went back to school and told my teacher, and she spoke to the principal. They told me to tell my foster parents that they'd let me go for free. (I guessed one of them would pay.) They also left voice messages on the phone and sent slip after slip. But my foster parents still refused to let me go, and the messages were deleted, even though it wouldn't have cost them a cent. All they had to give was their permission.

My two best friends at that time were Cedric and Abel. We all had our faults—Cedric had horrible breath, Abel's penmanship was horrible, and I lived in a horrible home. We tried to help each other. Cedric and I worked with Abel in trying to get him a grade higher than a C or D in penmanship. Abel and I were trying to tell Cedric what he needed to do to make his breath better. I was the only one who couldn't be helped by his friends. That was what I believed at that time, but I now see that they helped me emotionally. They were among the reasons why I loved school. Another was Vanessa, a girl in my class whom I had my first crush on. Cedric and Abel would tell her that I liked her and she would look at me and make wisecracks about me around her friends. But in class she would look at me and smile. I was confused because her behavior changed like that. One discovery about females was made in that classroom. (At that time it was a discovery.)   While we were doing math one day, a girl in the back raised her hand wildly, screaming that she had to use the bathroom. She was running up the aisle and stopped next to my desk when—uh oh, too late. She had a skirt on and I guess she wasn't wearing panties, because her urine was a stream, and it squirted backwards. I thought that was weird. The best times of my stay with Aunt Sable and Prizna were at school.

Then came that one dreadful day that completely turned me into an unbeliever in working foster homes. I think it was March 5, 1995, and I was on my way to school when I saw Cedric's mother driving him to school in their car. Cedric saw me, I asked if I could get a ride with them, and his mother told me to come on. I looked left and right and the coast was clear; the light was yellow but there were no oncoming cars. I started running and was almost across the street when a car hit me, I bounced off a parked car, my head hit the curb, and I lay there unconscious. When I came to, Cedric's mother was shaking me, crying and screaming for me to wake up. My lip was busted, my teeth were gone or had been pushed up in my gums, and I was dizzy and light-headed. Someone called an ambulance and my foster parents, and the first people on the scene were my teacher and principal. (This is why I think they cared more.) Some people may have thought that I lived farther away than I did, because nobody else was ther for me. But no, I was seven at that time and was only two to five minutes walking distance from my foster parents' house. I could sit on that street and literally look over at their house. But they had already left for work; a message was sent to them, but they didn't come until after my surgery. My principal went back to the school, but my teacher stayed with me. Then finally, Aunt Sable came and got me.

I know this was the end of my stay because later on that night Prizna told me I had to clean the floor one more time. I figured, what's one more time, so I got down on the floor and waited for that horrible smell and the aftermath. I was surprised that the smell wasn't bad at all—it actually smelled good, and I liked it. Then again, I had come to respect Prizna. That was the first time she'd seen me clean, and even then I was coughing. I think she could tell that I was having a tough time cleaning the floor. So, she left the room and came back with a mop and told me to get up and she would finish it. She was the only one to let me watch TV and that was when her sister wasn't home, and it was one time. I didn't care—she let me, and to me that was enough to earn my respect for her. She bathed me well that night, and the next day I was heading out. I never had the chance to thank my teacher or principal.

FAMILY TWO
The Skythes of Roselle

Silvia and Vinton Skythe were Christians and did many activities with their church. Silvia wanted me to call her Mom and her husband said to call him Vinton or whatever I wanted. I was moved to the Skythes because of the accident when I was seven. To tell you the truth, this home wasn't as bad as the previous one, because I actually had good times here. Also while I was here I was diagnosed with attention deficit/hyperactivity disorder (ADHD) and prescribed Ritalin for it. My first day there was fun; I had a pretty big room with a television, a work desk, and a dresser drawer. I searched the entire room to see what was different it compared to where I was previously. I didn't really know what Old Spice was until I saw this cologne and I used it a lot because it smelled good. In fact, I used the whole bottle. So, one day my foster mom asked, "What is that smell?" Then she looked over to me and I gave her a smirk, and right away she knew what was up and said, "I know your senses are impaired because mine are shot!" So I stopped using the cologne because I didn't know how much to use. The Skythe family took me with them to church every Sunday and I used to fall asleep every time.

Not long after I was with the Skythes, my mom noticed that I didn't have any front teeth. One day she asked me whether they were going to grow in eventually. I told her that I didn't know and that I had gotten hit by a car. Soon afterwards she took me to a dentist, who told her that I would need dentures or a partial. I didn't know what they were talking about; I was too busy getting stickers and candy. At the next visit the dentist took a mold of my mouth so that he could make the teeth. On the ride home that day I told my mom that I looked like a vampire, and she looked at me and laughed. Then finally I got my dentures, and the dentist told me I had to take care of them. I had to put them in solution every night, and he gave me a little blue container. He also told me to rinse my mouth out after eating so that food didn't stay on them. Lastly, he told me not to chew sugary gum because it would only to stick. So from then on I wore false teeth.

Every Friday night I always looked forward to Vinton picking me up from the after-school daycare center because he would take me to Bible Study with him. I'd always try to pay attention to what was being said, but usually within a half hour I was sleep. When we'd go to the study in Jersey City, we'd always stop at the Mexican-Jamaican Restaurant. We took out an order of my favorite, beef-stuffed plantain and/or Jamaican beef patty.

I had two neighborhood friends, Courtney and Zach, and we had tons of fun together. We went to each other's house and played games in each other's yard. In the event that I had to stay close to home, we spent a lot of time in Zach's yard, since he lived next door. One day while we were there, I was looking at Courtney, whom I had a little crush on. I said to her, "I sure wish there was a black girl that looked like you, because you are really cute." She giggled and said the same for me, and Zach got jealous and ran into his house.

My first day at my new school, Charles Polk School, was terrible, and I was picked on in second grade by the taller kids every day. I didn't do very well in the class because the bullies were always bothering me. I always retaliated against them, and every time I was removed. The school board met and the child study team decided that Special Ed would be best for me. So they placed me in Mrs. Truman's class, where I met my first girlfriend, Ivera Pierre. The class was nice and small, with about ten students and two teachers.

On a Friday in September, my class had a birthday party for me. On Saturday my family held a small family party for me too, allowing Courtney, Zach, and my other friend Biff to join me. We played games and ate cake and ice cream. Then my parents took us outside to the front of the garage, and as the door raised, my eyes lit up. Standing there was my brand new bike, the first one I had ever had. Courtney and Zach had to go home, but I had to try out my new bike. My parents told me how to ride and my mom held on to the seat as I pedaled, and then she released me. There were many days that I rushed my homework to ride my bike. On the weekends I used to speed up my chores and ride. I used to be lonely when Zach and Courtney couldn't ride with me. Nothing could separate me from my bike, until one day. It was a Saturday if I remember; I was riding my bike down a street I usually didn't go to, and I was being bold. As I was riding I started to go too fast and then I steered too far to the right. I rode right into a bush and got a stinging surprise. A bee had stung me right under my eye and I looked as though I had just fought Lennox Lewis. I forgot all about that bike and ran home, leaving it in the driveway of the old man who lived there. I never did find out who brought it back to me. When I went into the house, my mom told me to stop all my crying and she gave me some ice. The rest of the evening we watched the earlier version of *The Passion of the Christ* by Mel Gibson.

The day that changed everything was when I went grocery shopping with my mother. I reverted back to my thievery ways. We were at a ShopRite supermarket. At the cash register, I asked for a pack of Mentos and she said no. So I took them and put them in my pocket. As we were leaving, my mom was pushing the cart and I lagged behind. After we packed the trunk up, she told me to put the cart back. On my way back I started to run and she was looking right at me and the Mentos flew out of my pocket. Her mouth was wide open but she was speechless. I said immediately, "Wow! Mom, look what I found!" I ran to the Mentos and brought them to her. She asked if I had stolen them from the store and I told her no, and she slapped me in the mouth. Furious, she literally dragged me back to the store, and I was crying and screaming because I knew what was going to happen. She brought me in and spoke with the manager, telling him what I'd done, and I had to give the Mentos back. On the ride home she smacked me in the mouth every time I cried. She said, "Keep on crying and I'll just keep on smacking you," while I cried and tried to apologize at the same time.

Once we got home she told me to go upstairs and take off my pants and underwear and wait for her in my room.

I cried all the way upstairs. I pulled my pants down halfway and she came into the room with a belt. I started to back away from her with my hands up, crying and pleading for her to let me keep my underpants up. She then screamed and told me to pull them down. As I did so, she beat me until my behind and some of my private area was numb. It hurt so bad that I couldn't sit down. She told me to sit outside the living room and write down a hundred times "I will not steal." Then Vinton came home and saw me crying and writing and he told his wife she shouldn't beat me like that. She explained what I had done and he told her, "Even so, he's a child and there are other ways to discipline. Besides you aren't supposed to beat these kids, you know that." They slept in separate rooms. All I knew was that Vinton slept downstairs in his study room, and his wife slept in the regular bedroom.

As time went on I met my new in-home therapist, Arlene Machintosh. Arlene came down to the house once a week and brought games for us to play, and for Christmas she brought me the game "Sorry." She then left for her winter recess. For awhile I was pondering the idea of reporting Silvia Skythe. I was already used to regular beatings, but the one that followed the Mentos incident was the first time I'd had to pull down my underwear and be beaten like that. Usually I'd have to lie across the bed; this had been on an entirely different level. But, on the other hand, I was getting things that I never had before. I had my own room, television, a game system, movies, a queen-sized bed, and even a desk to do my homework and Bible study on. That was what really stopped me from reporting Silvia to Arlene.

We had a Christmas party two days before Christmas Eve. Me and my cousins Antoine, Tiffany, and Vanessa went to my room to watch movies and play while the adults were fellowshipping. We were jumping on my bed while watching *A Goofy Movie* and trying to reenact what they were doing. Once Antoine and Tiffany left, Vanessa and I were kissing for about five to ten seconds. Once we were done I asked why we did that, she said because I was cute and we weren't real family. Then Tiffany and Antoine returned and we were all jumping on the bed again and then there was a loud bang. We fell while trying to do what Max was doing in *A Goofy Movie*. My mom was furious—she hollered for us to get downstairs. My cousins were spanked, and I saw my mom looking at me, so I headed back upstairs. But she surely followed and beat me pretty bad; not like before, but bad. I got in bed and cried myself to sleep.

Later on that night my mom awakened me. She was sitting at the desk with the lamp on. She told me to get up and get on my knees because she wanted to show me how to pray. She taught me a prayer that seems pretty common now, seeing as a lot of people know it. "Lord, lay me down to sleep, and if I die before I wake, I give you Lord my soul to take. Amen." Then I got back in bed after she apologized, and I went to sleep. One of the things I accomplished besides learning to pray was that I was baptized.

Not long after I had prayed, I was awakened again, this time to leave to go down south, I believe to South Carolina. The trip was fun; we rode in Vinton's new '95 Lincoln Continental. On the way we made a few stops, one of which was to pick up a game called "UNO." My mom and I played it, and that was fun. We slept in the car because Vinton did not want Silvia to drive it. We arrived at Vinton's parents' house, where my grandpa and grandma were very welcoming on the first meeting. They gave me three Matchbox car cities and a pair of dress socks, as well as some fireworks. Grandpa, Vinton, and myself went out to light the firecrackers. I had such a wonderful time. The ride back was just as eventful as the way there, and we arrived back home at around two or three the third day, which was Christmas morning. Walking into the house, I saw the foot of the Christmas tree filled with a slew of gifts, both wrapped and unwrapped.

The next year my mom took me to my cousin Antoine's house to stay the night because they were going to the Six Flags amusement park the next morning. At Six

Flags I had the worst time of my life, because I was too short to go on any real good rides. I vowed never to go again. Antoine then stayed at my house for a night because my mom was taking us to Outdoor World. When we went, we had loads of fun. One time my mom told us to stay put and not get dirty, and she would be right back. She left and we ran off and got dirty. We were trying to wash it off before she got back, but no luck, and, yup, we got a whipping.

After that, I felt enough was enough. I said to myself that I was going to tell Arlene about what was going on. And that's what I did. Arlene went back to her office and filed the necessary paperwork to have me removed. Before leaving the Skythes, I finished school and I even got to kiss Courtney goodbye.

FAMILY THREE
The Banks of Roselle

Moving in with Mrs. Sharonda and Preston Banks was a special time for me, because I met my second girlfriend while I was with them. I lived in the house with three others, Mrs. Sharonda, Preston, and her son, Joe, who was seventeen and had two snakes, Dollar Bill and Crème. I loved to watch Joe feed his snakes the little mice. I wasn't with the Banks for very long.

Every day I went to summer daycare at the same place I had gone to from my previous home. My foster brother, Joe, was heading out one night to a party while I was watching a Care Bears movie, *Bears to the Rescue.* Then Sharonda sent me to bed. I was Joe's roommate and I woke up when he came in. Before he entered the house he vomited outside and came in stumbling and causing a lot of commotion, and his words were slurred. I overheard him talking to a friend, saying, "Aw, man, son, I was riding my bike home, high as hell, and I hit a parked car!" He was laughing and everything.

The next morning after Sharonda had left for work and Preston was out of the house, Joe and I were left. He had a backpack and was heading out, and he said he was heading to a friend's house to watch a movie on a tape he had with him. I was curious as to what types of things older kids watched, so I asked him what the movie was about. Joe popped the tape into the VCR and there was a lady making noises and sucking on something. I immediately said, "Ewe! Is that a hotdog?" Joe said no, it's a dick. At that moment the camera moved down to show a man lying on his back. I said, "*Yuck!* Take it out!" Before Joe left, he made me promise to not tell anyone. I told him sure, as long as he never showed me that tape again; it was nasty. I went to the kitchen for some cereal and turned the TV on to my favorite show, *Care Bears*.

Preston came in with perfect timing because my show was over. He told me to come to the basement to find a bike. All the bikes were either broken or too small for me. There was a pink power wheel Corvette, which I chose to play with instead. My friend Marcus and I played with the Corvette, pushing it around on the little dead end street next to my house.

Moments later Sharonda pulled up, then Preston and

Joe came out and I had to put the Corvette away. Preston told me that we were going to his mom's house. We arrived at his mother's house and they introduced me to her, but I forgot her name the minute she told me. Preston took me to the garage to show me something. Once he opened the garage, I saw a bunch of old-looking junk. He rummaged through the junk and worked his way somewhere near the back, from where he produced an old pink bike with a banana seat. The bike looked like it was from the '80s, and Preston told me it was mine now. He said he would get some new inner tubes for it, polish the metal, and get new petals. He told me that once it was all fixed I could ride anywhere I wanted. I looked happy, but deep inside I was embarrassed for the both of us—for him because I couldn't believe he had ridden a bike like that, and me because I was expected to.

After we arrived back home, Marcus was there waiting for me, so I pulled out the car and we started playing. As we were playing, there were some kids around the corner jumping on a trampoline. Among them was a pretty girl, and my eyes lit up and locked on her. Her name was Monica and she became my new girlfriend. There was construction being done on the short street next to my house, and they always left the Caterpillar. They were working on the road and the new sewage pipe line. The tractor became our meeting spot, where we talked and kissed and played with each other. The first time we French kissed for a long time, maybe about twenty seconds, I would jump onto the fence like Spiderman. We met there every day and every day started something different but ended with the Spiderman act. On our last "date" I picked her up and carried her out of sight, under the fence where the bushes were. It was then where we played with each other a little more. I use the word "play," because the intent wasn't strong enough to be a full-fledged sexual relationship. I didn't know this was our last date until the next day when she told me she was going out with someone else. It didn't bother me as a child because I knew it wouldn't have lasted. I was upset at that moment and then I got over it because "shit happens," right? That same day my friend Marcus and I went to my house and watched *Care Bears* and *Sesame Street* and ate pizza. Tom told me that he, Joe, his brother, and their girlfriends were going through the tunnel, and asked me if I wanted to come. I said yes.

The next day Marcus and I were watching *Care Bears* again, waiting for the other kids to come get us. Joe came down and walked out saying that he was going to get Tom, Marcus's brother. So we waited some more. About fifteen minutes later we went out and saw them heading toward the tunnel. We yelled, "Wait up!" and ran down to meet them. Joe said that he told us to come on when he was outside, because he was waiting for us. When we got down there, we saw two more girls and three more guys. The girls thought it was cute for them to bring their younger brothers.

As we entered the new tunnel, it was pitch black and some of the guys had flashlights. As we walked we saw water on the ground, some rats, and a few cats. While we were walking through the tunnel, the older kids were kissing and hugging their girlfriends. They were also saying things to them that didn't sound appropriate to me. Back behind us the light that was there disappeared, and not too long after we were in the tunnel, we heard a noise behind us. I think there were two other beams of light behind us and we started running, and I mean we were out the gate. The older kids were going at full speed and we were trying to stay close enough that we didn't see the lights. Then we ran into Joe and the others. Joe told us to run in front of them because he'd gotten scared for a moment that he'd lost us. The guys behind us were screaming and we ran even faster and we saw some light at the other end of the tunnel. Our first step back outside was in a stream of water. It wasn't brown or dark colored, but actually clear and in the middle of the street. We climbed the ladder and I saw that we were only six blocks from home. Joe told me to go home because he and his friends were going to their friend Jessica's house. The rest of us said we had to do it again. As we were heading to my house I noticed that the tunnel was really nothing but a big curve.

About an hour later Sharonda walked in with Preston, Joe, and her daughter Janice, who was in college. Marcus had to go home because the rest of us were going to see the new house Sharonda was about to buy. We drove to Spruce Street, which wasn't far from our old house, which was by coincidence also on a Spruce Street. This "new" Spruce Street wasn't considered real because it was a dead end and consisted of only two houses. Besides, we received our mail on Chapel Avenue. When we arrived at our new house, it was beautiful. It had two floors. The upper floor had two bedrooms and one bathroom in the master suite and a bathroom in the hall for the other room. There was a nice-sized kitchen, a dining room, and a small area where she could put the "Don't touch" furniture. This first floor area was considered the basement although it was finished. We had a television in our room and next to our room there was the family room, where we kept our games. There was a linen closet down the hall before the bathroom, and there was the garage door directly down the hall from our room. At this house we had an even bigger backyard and a little brick patio. We rode home that day all smiles and said we couldn't wait to make that move. Within a week we were packed up and ready to go.

As soon as we arrived at the new house, Joe and I set up our stuff in our room and put our clothes in the closet and bureau and still had space left over. Joe set up the side wall with the cubicle shelves and his snake cage. Then, lastly, our bunk bed was moved in. The dining room had two large china closets. The kitchen was packed with fairly new appliances, including a microwave, trash compactor, refrigerator, and dishwasher. The Banks packed it with new dishes and pans. We had our first garage, which was filled with the things we used to keep in the basement at the old house, and we still had enough room left over for the car. The Banks had sold their old house to the church behind it, because it had needed a fellowship hall.

Throughout the last two weeks of August I couldn't see or speak to my old friends, nor did I have anyone to play with. So I became creative and I made whips out of sticks, string, and a blade. I used this to cut grass, bushes, and beehives as I walked past them. Sharonda told me numerous times to not make them, but I did anyway. Every time I'd replace the whip Sharonda would twist my ear because she constantly told me to not make them. She didn't want me to get hurt.

Shortly after I became integrated into this new home, my real mother, Crystal, and her husband, my stepdad, found out where it was. I saw them walking down the street while I was on the porch one day and I ran and hugged my mom. My stepdad had just got out of jail and had become a saved Christian. He listened to gospel music and he gave me his only Walkman and gospel tape. (I actually saved these things for years afterward, until I was about seventeen. That was my favorite tape; I hope to find another copy of it one day.) My mom told me I had to go back because they couldn't have me right then. The people who were watching me were Sharonda's sister and Preston. Seeing my mother that day really lightened my life and I wished so bad that I could be with her. At that moment I didn't care what she had done to me—I just wanted to be with her. I loved her so much and wished I could leave.

Not long afterward, I had a birthday party at school. My teacher, Mrs. Trumas, had a surprise for me; she told me that I was advancing to the harder class, with Mr. Rudwig. He was at the party too because his class was with the other teacher.

When I got home, Sharonda and her sister were there to greet me. When they opened the door I was welcomed with "Happy Birthday!", and a few others were there to greet me. When I got upstairs Sharonda told me to go into the living room. When I went in, my eyes lit up; they had bought me an army train. It had tracks, little men, a train, and a control unit. They also bought me a monster truck that drove by a stick on the top of it. I played with the monster truck in the backyard for hours.

I went to Mr. Rudwig's class the next day and saw my cousin Rochelle there and also my first girlfriend, Ivera. I felt different about her because she wasn't like other girls, maybe because she was Indian. We broke up before the summer and got back together in Mr. Rudwig's class. When we were together she never talked about sex like the other girls, she liked to take her time with things. I remember the first time we decided to kiss. She wrote a note on a big piece of construction paper: DO YOU WANT TO KISS ME? YES OR NO. Circle one. Then she passed it to me (I sat right in front of her) and I took it and circled yes. Then I wrote on the bottom: WHEN? Then I passed it back and she whispered that she didn't know. (In retrospect, I thought that was kind of cute how we did that.) So we ended up waiting until after school, where we met somewhere and kissed. I was so happy to be back with her in Mr. Rudwig's class, and even then when we were older, we still only kissed. Mr. Rudwig's class was different—we learned about horticulture, and the class had its own garden. I was now able to take part in planting tulip bulbs, sunflowers, and different vegetables: carrots, tomatoes, potatoes, peppers, egg plant, squash, and many others. We tended to the garden every time we went out, and it was fun because Ivera and I always found time to kiss.

When I came home Sharonda told me that I would be leaving soon and I began to cry and holler. She told me that I wouldn't go to school the next day but that I would be going to another home for an interview. I didn't see any reason why, because the Banks had never done anything bad to me. I went down to the family room and cried. I was wondering why they were taking me away from the best thing, next to my mother, in my life. I hated to have to go.

On the way to the interview, I didn't talk much at all because I was trying to ignore my caseworker. When we were heading up the driveway of the house, it was like climbing a hill, and the house looked like a hotel. I asked my caseworker if it was one, and he told me no. We were greeted by the housekeeper and she told us to come in and have a seat while she got the Edwins. I met Jim and he told me to call him Pop, so that was what I called him. I still remember the first time I saw this tall man; he picked me up and carried me out to his car with him. I was already growing attached. The overall interview went well and we were on our way back. Upon arriving back home I left the car and told Sharonda that I wanted to stay with her, because I didn't want to move anymore.

On my last day of school, Mr. Rudwig, Mrs. Trumas, and Mrs. Behr threw me a going-away party and I had donuts, juice, soda, pizza, and ice cream and cake. I was really going to miss Ivera and my cousin Rochelle. Mrs. Behr took a picture of me eating a donut with Ivera walking behind me, and of me with Mr. Rudwig and Ms. Trumas. The last picture taken was me and the entire class sitting in the back and Ivera was sitting next to me with her head on my shoulder. (I still have every one of these pictures.) I got one last kiss from Ivera before I never saw her or any of them again. I was moving on to a new home and new life once again.

The next day changed my life forever, when I was picked up by my caseworker and off we went.

FAMILY FOUR
The Edwins of Woodstown

Before going to this home I had to spend the night at someone's house. I don't quite remember their names because it was only one night. They had two children and they lived in a three-bedroom house. I slept in the guest room. In their home was a real arcade game, and the dad showed me how to play it. From that point on, I played the game non-stop, because it was my only comfort zone. For dinner we had breakfast. It was a surprise to me because this was the first time in my life that I had breakfast for dinner. I slept well and I was gone the next day.

The Edwins were to be my everlasting parents, my father Jim and my mother Van. They treated me like a son. You might have thought that I was made of gold, but gold can be replaced and a son can't. They loved me even during the times when I was having adjustment problems.

That was part of their greatness.

I arrived to live with them on October 18, 1996. Pop was getting ready for a funeral. I asked him if I could ride the little Kettcar and he told me to wait until their son got home because it was his. Then he left. So I went upstairs and asked Mrs. Edwin if I could ride the Kettcar and she said, yes. Jim pulled up because he had forgotten something and as he was leaving he caught me riding the Kettcar. He told that he'd said no and for me to get off and leave it alone. I then told him that Mrs. Edwin had said I could ride it. He said that if he told me no and I went and asked somebody else, that was called "manipulation," and I shouldn't do that. I said okay and went back into the house. They taught not only that what you did was wrong but *how* it was wrong. They ran a teaching family program. When I came to live with the Edwins, I had to start counseling and see a psychiatrist for my medication.

Later on that first day, the Edwins' other children came home, and the first one to greet me was Rawuu Napaul. He grabbed my bags, showed me to my room, helped me put my clothes away, and took me on a full tour of the house. I was amazed to see that I was on a farm, the first one I had ever really seen, let alone lived on. There were chickens, emus, goats, horses, cows, turkeys, guinea pigs, ducks, geese, pigs, peacocks, roosters, hens, and a swan. A majority if not all had little chicks. They had a huge satellite dish which moved by remote control, and tons of nice cars which changed over the years; some stayed, some went, and some were remade. The house was round like a donut and it had a bubble-dome window in the center of the roof. The house had two chimneys with a bell atop one, which was rung by a pull string. They had an in-ground pool that was heated and they had a lot of grills. Then we toured the inside of the house, which I basically knew, because I had been home all day. Overall, the home was beautiful, and it appealed to my taste because it was so different.

The living room was off-limits because every home had a room with the "Don't touch" furniture. The family room where we spent a lot of time looked very nice and it had the very first model of the big-screen television. It had to have projection in order to show a picture. There was a fold-out in front that looked like a backwards capital "L," on which was a mirror. When this was opened, it revealed red, green, and blue lights on the bottom of the TV which looked like horizontal traffic lights. These lights formed a picture and projected off of the mirror and onto the screen. It sounds complicated, but it was simple. The kitchen and dining room really fascinated me because, once again, this was the first time I had ever seen a wall completely covered with a mirror. The kitchen had a full mirror wall. The dining room had a curved mirror wall. From the bottom floor, you could see every room on the second floor. I could stand in the living room and look up into a bedroom. This was weird for me, but nowadays it's becoming a little more common in new home developments. After the tour, I met Lance and Shawn and their son Fanden, who became my best friend and brother.

It took almost a month before I was able to start school. My first teacher at Mary Shoemaker Elementary School was Mr. Walton. I was in the fourth grade. I had a lot of fun in class, and the kids and teacher were welcoming. I felt older and smarter because I got to move around to go to different classes. I had to go to gym, art, music, the library, and to the computer lab. My days at school were pretty simple.

There were two girls in my class who sat next to me and annoyed me a lot, but they became my friends. One girl was Raychelle, who often wore knee-high socks and an old-fashioned skirt to school, and the other was Danuelle. They kept playing games and calling me "master." So I told Raychelle to keep it up and I'd slap her, and she kept it up just to see what I would do. She didn't know me, I was the new kid, remember—so I slapped her. The school provided the students with behavioral cards that had faces on them to show how a student's behavior had been on a given day. I received a sad face because I hit Raychelle.

Heading home, I looked at the card and began to feel scared because my mother used to beat me over cards like this. I brought it home anyway, because my brother was nowhere to be found so he could throw it away for me.

Mrs. Edwin was very disappointed over what I had done. After speaking with me, she helped me understand that it was wrong. She also learned that I never knew a boy couldn't hit a girl. Mrs. Edwin told me to apologize the next day in front of the class and have my teacher make a note of it in writing. She sent a note to school with me the next day. I had received time-out in a "thinking room" for hitting Raychelle. The school's disciplinary system allowed three thinking rooms and then a detention. A thinking room meant no recess—instead we had to write what we had done and how it was wrong, and after we finished we had to do dictionary pages.

The rest of my time at school went very well. I didn't receive another thinking room all year. On the last day of school, the other students in my class each received a recorder from the music teacher, but I didn't. I asked for one and she told me that I had come too late, because the other students had already learned how to play it. I it was heartbroken and cried. The last hour of the day Mr. Walton sent me to Mrs. Snodgrass's class, where she was standing in the doorway waiting for me with a recorder in her hand. She told me that the instructions were inside and for me to have fun. I thanked her so much that I gave her a big hug.

We lost Napaul—I think he went crazy or something; after we came back from Cancun, he ran away. On his way out he hit one of my older foster brothers, Durh, with a huge tree limb. Then my other foster brother Tah grabbed him, but Pop said to let him go. They did and he ran down the hill, and my parents called the police. Shawn had run away as well, and was heading to his home in Trenton. My foster brothers found him walking along the highway.

Around late 1997, shortly after I turned nine, something happened to me that changed my life. A new kid came into the home named Homer, from Paterson, New Jersey. He was my roommate and kept showing me weird things he had learned. I always walked away because I thought it was odd. Then one day he kept begging me to play this game with him and I gave in to it because he was being annoying. This game led to other odd games, and I kept asking him was it right and he said it was only a game. One night while I was home and he was away with his mom, I decided to sleep on the floor because it was cooler. My mom was in her office late that night when Homer returned. He came into the room and forcefully penetrated me, and I woke up crying and screaming. My mom came out of her office and asked what was wrong and I told her. She made Homer sleep out in the hallway, while I slept in the bedroom. My mom then took us to counseling the next week and we saw a therapist, Mrs. Maurine Ingall. She interviewed us about what was happening and I told everything that I had participated in. My mom explained to her that I didn't have a history of sexual incidences.

I started getting counseling for what had happened and I began to pull through, though it has always had a lasting effect. Homer, on the other hand, was getting worse. My mother, the strong woman she was, tried to help him and support him, and she had him attend many sexual treatment groups. During the time Homer was receiving this treatment and starting to change his ways for the better, a new kid came in, Quan Chi Goodwill, who became Homer's roommate. Soon after, Homer had him in some mess. Then my foster brother Shawn was soon removed because he was being inappropriate with our dog.

I was rooming with Lance and he knew all that was going on. One morning after we ate breakfast, we had to clean our room and he came upstairs and turned off the light. He walked up to me and told me to "suck his dick." When I told him no, he grabbed my head and forced his penis into my mouth, and I almost vomited. So I bit it and he released my head and I told Pop and he called a family conference. Quan Chi and Lance were removed and later down the line (when I was twelve) Homer was also removed, after he hit a new kid, Mart, in the face and sent him to the emergency room.

During 1998 Fanden and I started dance class; we were taking tap and jazz. As time went on we started taking hip-hop classes. Eventually I was promoted to the competition team after my friend Jay. I was upset that he got it before me, because he had started after I had. I decided that I should try a little harder and I earned it in 2001, my first year of high school. What I was missing was the fact that you had to earn it; they didn't just give it to you for having good attendance. So I asked my dance teacher if she could put me in the harder class. I remember the song to my first advanced class dance: "Cars."

After the competition team in high school, I took more classes and spent hours of devotion and working on my solos. I attended Eastern Dance Studio in Penns Grove and Swedesboro, New Jersey. The people there were friendly but got serious when it came time to get down to business. My dance teacher was a great resource for me, especially when I started my dance solos. My first competitive performance was at the Sophisticated Dance Competition in Plymouth Meeting, Pennsylvania. We were doing a boy's tap and we won High Gold for this dance. To make a long story short, I have won over fifteen awards and trophies for dance (along with trophies for other activities). I met some amazing people at this dance studio, and they still serve as motivation to me today.

Before all of the crazy things started happening at the Edwins' home, we used to have fun. When there were older kids there, I had to learn quickly that tattle-telling on simple things was annoying to people. As soon as I learned that, I adjusted very well to the home. Durh watched the kids during the week for our parents because they were busy. We always loved going to Mr. Guymon's house on the weekends because we knew we'd see Dondy. Durh's friend Dondy worked there like Durh worked at the Edwins. Needless to say, we spent a lot of time there, especially in the summer after summer camp. On Fridays we'd go to the movies sometimes or skating.

On the weekends we had to go to the Guymons, who also ran a teaching family program. We went there on the weekends to give Mom and Pop a break from the week. Here we had loads of fun. Mr. Guymon's wife, Bedy, took us out to a lot of places. We went to the mall, movies, skating rink, parks, and parties or barbecues. This was almost like a home away from home.

Mr. Guymon was the pastor of a church in Rosenhayn, New Jersey. He had many barbecues and game events. We played basketball tournaments at a park across the street from the church, and he hosted volleyball tournaments. I was a great server.

When I turned twelve I had been defeated and yet saved. God had worked through these loving people and given them the strength to break down my barriers. I couldn't have done it without them, and we couldn't have done it without God. I could no longer lump all foster homes together, because the Edwins were a different breed. They didn't beat the barriers down with a belt or stick; nor did they ignore me and think they'd come down by themselves. No, they tore them down with love. They loved me and I loved them for that; they cared for me, they helped me through my hard times, and they took me through the good fight.

My parents felt that it was time I learned to be more responsible for myself. They taught me how to cook, clean, and be thorough when completing a responsibility. My dad taught me how to do landscaping work, to plant trees, flowers, and gardens, and cut grass. He taught me how to put together a waterfall or fountain outside and how to take care of animals and such. He took me to his job. He is a funeral director and owns Edwards and Sons Funeral Homes, Inc., in Bridgeton and Salem, New Jersey. He showed me how the process went in his job, both the physical and the business part. He exposed me to the working atmosphere; he had me be a part of many funerals. My parents shaped me into the ideal worker with motivation and dedication. They shaped me into a reliable family man, with cooking, cleaning, landscaping, and problem-solving skills.

Just when everything was going so well in my life, DYFS entered the picture from out of nowhere. They were trying to get me adopted and I began to feel afraid, worried, confused, and very upset. They always did this to me: They waited until I was in a home that I liked and in which I was doing well, and then they took me away. They kept videotaping me and taking me to events, almost like an auction where there were parents all over trying to pick the ideal child. I was being interviewed and then I became scared that I may leave. What really made me upset was when I learned they wanted to put me in a home with two men. Two dads? This really didn't sit well with me at all, because I couldn't say anything. It felt like: Throw him anywhere, as long as he's no longer our concern.

During this time, I was in perpetual turmoil. School was a struggle, I had frequent suspensions, and my grades had dropped a little; for the first time, I was worried about failing or getting anything lower than a "B" on my report card. I also learned my first sexual game in school, which I played at home; and then I realized that it was more wrong than I'd thought. Then I had to go to the psychiatrist, where he changed my medication from Ritalin to Concerta 54 milligrams and Zyprexa 2.5 milligrams twice a day. Initially the Concerta was 36 milligrams and the Zyprexa was 5 milligrams at night. I was on these medications from early eighth grade to the year I graduated high school. This medicine had "zombiefied" me from the inside, although it didn't seem to affect me much on the outside. I felt emotionally dismissed from that day on.

One day I went out to the garage and saw the peacocks on the expensive car scratching it up. I grabbed a broom and started swinging at them and they all ran out. Little did I know that one had slid under the refrigerator and another one could not eat. I never knew that I had hit any; I had just been swinging until they'd left. It affected me a lot because I loved the peacocks, and it hurt to know that I had done that.

My parents saw that what DYFS was doing was causing problems with my sense of security, so they saved me from the stress. They called DYFS and told them that they want them to stop the interviews for me, because they were going to keep me forever.

Years and years of the same thing went by until two events happened, a happy one and an unhappy one. The happy event was that Durh got married to Dee and they had a beautiful horse-and-carriage wedding at the house.

The yard was filled with cars, the hill was filled with cars, and I drove the golf cart around to get the handicapped people. Unfortunately I missed his wedding because I had a dance recital to go to that day. The unhappy event was the separation of the Guymons, who went their separate ways. Going to Mr. Guymon's house didn't seem the same anymore. The dogs that ran around were gone, and that funny, smiling Mrs. Bedy wasn't around anymore. Things just seemed to change and I began to get worried because I felt like everything was going down.

I set myself one main goal while I am on earth, besides to follow God, and that is to eventually become a cardiovascular surgeon. My parents supported my decision and I've had this game plan since I was in the eighth grade. I am determined to do it, and I am going to try.

As my life went on and things at times got too much for me to handle, I would at times feel depressed, and many times I would pray to God and ask him to bring me home. I would never commit suicide, because, first of all, I love myself too much, and, secondly, God forbids it. Yet, the pain I would feel was so real, and it didn't go away that quickly. At one point, I had lost all hope for life and what I wanted to do in it, because I was trapped and I didn't know how to get out. I resorted to inappropriate sexual behaviors, and I engaged my younger foster brother in them. Eventually, the court system got involved with my sexual behaviors and sent me to a program to gain more understanding of myself.

There was a woman who came to the house to interview me about the incident. She looked just like my foster brother. They were caucasion, blond hair and blue eyes. When she was through interviewing him she called me in. She never asked me my side of the story. I had no intention of lying about any of it. She scolded me and made me feel as though I was dirt; at the time I didn't feel I deserved that. Her name was Mrs. Rumsfeld and she was a forensic doctor.

When she first came she told me that I wouldn't be prosecuted and that I wouldn't go anywhere. She told me that I had high dreams and a pretty solid future planned for myself and that I would be able to finish high school. She later reneged on her initial statement and filed charges and ruined my life and I didn't know how I would go on. I was so afraid because I had never gotten into trouble and this was beyond trouble. I didn't know what I would do. At the end of the day it was Mr. Frugal's decision as well. He was the director of the Devereux program and he reneged on his word as well. It felt like a quick scheme to end the succession in my life. I had won so many awards and now this.

Through the whole court process my main "main advocates" weren't there. I can remember one day while I was outside my parents room and they called me in. I saw them crying and very upset. The look on my face may have seemed as though it wasn't phasing me, but deep down inside it was tearing me apart. They asked me to close the bedroom door. Then my mom had broke it to me, "DiPetri, you have ___nobody___, no mother, no father, no Devereux, and no **DYFS.** All you have is us. But don't worry baby, we gon' take care of you." In between her words, there were snorts and cries. My dad was lying down on the other side and he was crying and I had wanted to drop dead at that time.

Meanwhile, I completed the court-ordered treatment program to correct my inappropriate sexual behaviors very successfully, without having any problems or relapses into those sexual incidents. The staff there really helped me a lot—especially my therapist and my mentor. My mentor always told me that as long as I kept being good, the way I was, he wouldn't have to work as hard. Overall he taught me a lot and I thanked him for it. He helped me out to understand that I don't need to change my basic self. Instead, it is also up to others to learn to adapt to me as I am. All the staff was exceptional—they had to be from the start because it takes a lot to work in a place like that. I know because it took a lot to live there. Try to picture going home every day with the kids in your class. Nightmare. I can't lie: In my heart, I felt that the program was horrific, and I hated it. In reality, that was because it wasn't home.

When I had turned eighteen, the time came for me to leave the program. Guess who decided to jump back into my life?—the good old DYFS, which proceeded to do absolutely nothing but bring back my past fears of going to another foster home. I never had a say in the choices that determined my future, aside from the negative things I did. I couldn't explain to any of those bureaucrats and office workers how I felt, but I knew that I had been hindered for far too long and that it was time for me to take a stance. For so much of my life I have felt powerless to make any relevant decisions about where I want to be, what I want to do. I have always known what I wanted and what the best choices were for me, but the thought that stuck out most was, "I have no control." It hurt so bad to know that my concerns weren't even taken into consideration. Through it all, GOD has pulled me through, my life is moving forward, and in the end I WILL PREVAIL. Because it was God's will, I am still here today.

As time progressed I outgrew my ADHD. I currently don't take any medications and I am making it very well. I am a healthy, self-controlled, smart, law-abiding citizen.

Thank you for listening to my story. I hope everyone who has read this will understand its content and meaning, because something must be done. I know that I am not the only person who has lived a life like this. Please, I encourage all of those who have had similar problems: Speak out.

Part II

THE SYSTEM

Lost and Trying to Find the Way

I want people to know how DYFS affects the youths it removes from their homes, and how little DYFS knows about these children. I am speaking mainly for the children who are able to understand what's happening. DYFS will put a child in a foster home not knowing how he or she will be treated. DYFS doesn't have any regard as to how the child may feel living in the home or even leaving his or her own home.

In DiPetri's first home, the old aunt treated him like dirt, and he even tried to get away, but she pulled him back. In all the other homes, DiPetri hadn't once tried to run away. He wouldn't have been there long enough for that accident to happen if DYFS had visited him at least once. There was no way DiPetri could've called them; that woman wouldn't have allowed it, and he was only six. Besides, no one told him that he could call DYFS. He thought he was there forever.

They then placed DiPetri into a home that beat him. DYFS did step it up a little and gave him a therapist, which was probably for his accident, when he got hit by a car. The family treated him pretty well, although there were beatings, but he was used to those, so that didn't affect him too much. He was also coming from a very unfortunate lifestyle, and the things they provided were beyond what he was used to. He was also able to have friends and go out into the neighborhood—he felt normal. This was something good for him. No DYFS. Maybe he should have gone out and gotten hit by a car again, only this time it would be on purpose. Maybe DYFS would be first on the scene and he could the caseworker how normal he felt. Silvia had always beaten that poor kid so much that he finally had to tell his therapist. The previous home had taken away all of his trust in foster families, but just when he thought he could give them another chance, this home was another setback. His trust in homes was definitely shot, and no more would he see them as being good again. No more would he call foster parents Mom and Dad. No more would he mingle with the parents or the family. "It's me, myself, and I," he thought.

The next home was better. They treated him well. His wonderful therapist bought him a dog on her last day, which he named Tom, after his oldest brother. This home was working out well; he had grown very attached to the family and felt as though he could live there. Once again, DYFS never showed to ask him anything, and just moved him. He never knew why, but he thought it was because his biological mother had found out where he lived. He didn't even want to move—in this home he had his freedom and his individuality. The parents weren't home all day and he was able to be his own person; besides, they never mistreated him.

The last home was the best he'd ever been in, yet it was here that he experienced many problems. The problems came in over conflicts between love, care, and concern versus individuality. Did DYFS know this? No! There were many times when DiPetri screwed up because of his severe and difficult problems, and most of the time, DYFS was there for those. But whenever he did anything good or needed something, it wasn't there when he could have used it. It was supposed to so-called "pay" for educational costs. But when asked to do so, it never came through once, and never reimbursed him or his foster families the money they paid for school supplies. When it was trying to have DiPetri adopted, he expressed his feeling that they were trying to dump him onto the highest bidder, but DYFS never heard him.

I think DYFS needs to be more consistent in the way it deals with its clients. Through my own experiences and observations, I know that a lot of juveniles seek negative attention. A lot of times when a juvenile commits a crime or misdemeanor or plans bad behavior, it is his or her way to get attention. Yeah, everybody knows that when you dig into the life of a child with behavioral problems, you find lack of attention and bad parents, among other factors. We don't need a psychiatrist or therapist to tell us that.

Where we are at fault is in not doing something about it. Very few parents teach their kids how to get positive attention. When a child gets attention only when he or she is being bad, the child sort of becomes conditioned to being bad to get what he or she needs. For example, a child comes home with A's and B's and tries to tell his mother about it, but she says she's busy. He goes downstairs and smacks his little brother until he cries and tells his mother. She comes down to scold her child, who apologizes and says, "Hey, Mom, I got A's and B's on my report card." She congratulates him and he moves on with his life. This is the only way the child learns to get attention.

There were other things that affected DiPetri while he was in his last home. He was on medication called Zyprexa, and it made me feel lousy. While he was taking this medication, he felt like he had no control over his emotions. It made him feel as though his feelings weren't there. This made it very difficult for him to express himself to others. The medicine was supposed to help him control his moods, which used to change frequently. The psychiatrist would always ask him how he was feeling on the medication, and he'd always say fine because he didn't feel any different. Medications should be tested to see if they are doing anything for the child, if the child is better or worse with or without the medication. This, for one, is something DYFS would have never known.

In my experience, DYFS doesn't have enough evidence to take a child from his family. Someone calls DYFS and says the parent is abusing the child and DYFS comes and takes the child. It needs to get as much proof and evidence as possible to take a child from his family. This makes a child emotionally disturbed. Especially if the child is old enough to recognize that he has parents and knows what they look like. This is something that puts a burden on the child and the parents. I bet DYFS has never asked the parents how they felt. To top it all off, DYFS puts the child in a home that it knows nothing about, to keep the child as far away as possible from his biological family—this at least was the case for DiPetri, even though he had very capable relatives that lived in other places; no, he had to be out of his mom's reach.

Lastly, I want to address the fact that DYFS doesn't include the child in any of the decisions it makes when it plans the child's life. When it was about to force DiPetri to live in a family run by two men, he was never consulted. That was wrong; a child shouldn't be subjected to participate in anything he doesn't want to. Two homosexuals may live together if they want to, but they should not put a child through that sort of transition. A child should be able to say whether he wants to make that move. Your environment can have a major effect on you in the aspect of changing your perceptions of things. DYFS did not include DiPetri in anything, and most of the time he wasn't ready to make these moves. Everything with DYFS is based on protecting itself against liability, not what's best for the child. It is playing with the stability of these kids' lives. How can an agency make the right decisions in a child's life unless it knows the child personally? His caseworkers didn't even know poor DiPetri's birthday. Even a little detail like that can cause so much trouble for a person down the line, if the person claims one birthdate and DYFS has him down for another—who do you think is going to be believed?

I have always wondered why DYFS hasn't tried to put children with relatives to help the biological parents out. If it's treatment they need, get a court order to put them there. If it's money, fund them and help them find jobs. If it's counseling, get it for them. As so on, but don't completely remove the kids from the families' lives. DYFS takes people's children away and gives them a time limit to heal before they get them back. Sometimes, things take longer than you think. Sometimes if a person is trying and that deadline is coming up, the person may ask for more time, but most likely will be denied. So it is almost like having to give up because kids are the main motivators and that's what gets most people by. DYFS never thinks that the parents might have feelings? This can be emotional on them too. There are a lot of factors that I feel DYFS is ignoring. It needs to stop abusing these children with its ignorance toward the child's feelings. Its staffs are what a mentor, my peers, and I like to call "the uninformed." These are the people who don't know what the children who are their clients go through. They don't know the child from what they read in his file and hear from the family. It's about time they started asking, and not when it's too late. A child can end up dead, and then liability is out the window. Hire more workers, make more visits, do what you need to step it up. Start asking!

One day DYFS will find out the truth about itself and its flaws. The story of DiPetri's life, I am hoping, will take people to the next level of child care and vigilance. I know you may be wondering how I know so much about DiPetri. Well, I know so much because I am DiPetri, and the author of this book. This was my life, this was my strife to take on and overcome.

Here's one of the poems that I wrote, I think it goes well with this subject:

(Something to think about the phrase):

I Know

I know there is a light at the end of the path
I know that forever it will not last
I know that in order for me to get answers I must follow
I know that in order for humility to set in I must swallow
My pride because
I know pride will hinder my ability to move
Forward
I know that the best way to go is forward because
I know that I can be a success
I know that, in what I do, I want to be the best
These are all difficult things to gain to be a success
Moreover, these are all simple in their own way
And others may ask am I sure,
I say sure I am, because I KNOW
But on the other hand do I?

- Jamil Ellison

EPILOGUE

A Little about the Author

Since I was six in May of 1994, I was taken from my biological family and since then I felt like I was on my own. Throughout my life I had to face so much emotional stress, and times when I was neglected, beaten, and taken for granted. These families held me back from so much, from so many things I could've done in life. From six to about twelve or thirteen, I was waiting for someone who never came. Never showed her face and I didn't know why. My mother never came, I don't know if she ever got well, and I hated her for it. I held up all these years, fighting off all these bad homes, thinking Mommy is coming to get me. I didn't need for these homes to like me, because I wasn't theirs to like. I cried every night that I didn't see her face. I used to get family visits every other Wednesday, and DYFS stopped them. I asked why and my caseworker never gave me a complete answer. Besides, I was a kid—what would I know about not having a family to see? I felt like I lost my mother forever. I remember when I was nine, I bought my mother Revlon makeup for Mother's Day. She took it and smiled, and that made me feel warm inside.

The time came when all the fighting and waiting stopped. I took on my current family as my family and I was convinced that I didn't want to see my mother again. Since nine or ten years old I haven't cried with any real feeling attached to it. In February 2006, a very significant someone who cared about my well-being told me I should go find my biological mother. The week before, on February 12, 2006, my mother had said the same thing and I had said flat-out no. But I became convinced that I should find her, because you only get one mother, and people make mistakes. The person who advised me helped me realize that I can't go on without finding some answers. With my change of heart and support from my family, I will go on to find my mother and continue to do well in life. I am still looking for the right one to complete my life. In persistence, I will go on and finish college in hopes that I become that cardiologist I want to be, then to one day reach my final long-term goal: to be a cardiovascular surgeon.